SOMETHING TO  THINK ABOUT

52 modern day parables

BY JIM COLLINS

Contents

Foreword

It is 10 years since I first began to work for the Herald Express, and even in this relatively short time, I've seen a marked decline in the amount of people expressing their faith on a regular basis.

During the same period, the From Your Parish page has gone from strength to strength. It is a home for all that is going on from the world of faith, and is one of the most popular pages of the paper.

I approached Jim in the glorious summer of 2012, as the Olympic spirit filled communities and truly brought them together.

People volunteered to serve their communities for free, laid on parties to celebrate the Jubilee. My memories are that there was an overwhelming sense of both pride and optimism. It was the summer in which I felt the country rediscovered its identity and place in the world.

Jim bottled that optimism with his writing, and has continued to do so ever since. His thoughts on whatever topic are now the cornerstone of the page, providing short, hugely readable thoughts on a vast array of subject matters.

And through the means of the paper, these words are able to reach a wide and diverse audience. Some of that audience might not have yet found their identity.

Enjoy Jim's thoughts, dip in to them and revisit when you can. Whether you are looking for optimism, a pathway, a sense of scale or perspective, you'll be joining a wider 'congregation' that has discovered his work.

Jon-Paul Hedge, Herald Express

Introduction

I moved from Reading to South Devon in 1979. Within a year of arriving, I met up with three other lads who were keen to form a band to share the Good News of the Gospel in music and song. It was during this time that I started to write down what I call – "modern day parables." I used some of these parables as introductions to songs when we played as a Band.

A parable by definition is a wise saying or a fictitious short story told to illustrate or highlight a spiritual or moral truth. Jesus used parables frequently – especially when he was speaking to crowds. He wanted to get the people thinking and to reflect on the kingdom of God.

The 52 modern day parables in this book (one for each week of the year) are made up of some of my life's experiences and observations – with a few topical thoughts added along the way. Each theme is then linked to the truth of the Bible – revealing that "God is able to make himself known in all things."

Wherever you are in your journey of life and walk of faith with God – I hope this book will give you "SOMETHING TO THINK ABOUT," and bring hope, encouragement and strength to you.

PS – If you think that it is "you" mentioned in any of these parables – thank you very much for your part towards inspiring me to write!

Jim Collins

New Year

It's amazing what we can do with the latest computer technology. Having said that, I have to admit I am not very adventurous in using it.

By using a computer you can order all your groceries on-line without seeing anyone, do all your banking tasks without speaking to anyone and get any information you like without relating to anyone.

I'm not against computer technology – but as I start a New Year I am reminded that I need to make and choose opportunities to make contact with people. (I still deliberately go into my bank to be served by a member of staff, even though I could use my card in the hole in the wall)

Shy people may find it hard to mix, and we all have times when we just want to be alone, but God made us to be a community of people and for community. (Living and sharing life together in social unity)

In Genesis, the first book in the Bible, Jacob said to Joseph that "God Almighty… had said to him… I will make you a community of peoples… (Genesis 48:3-4)

Jesus always made time for people: to meet them, and to meet their needs. In Luke 9:10-17, we read that Jesus was in Bethsaida, and He had spoken about the kingdom of God to the crowds that had followed him, and healed those who needed healing.

The apostles said to Jesus, "Send the crowd away so they can go into the surrounding villages and find food..." Jesus replied "You give them something to eat". (The feeding of the 5000 followed)

This New Year – ask God to help you go out of your way to speak and make contact with people.

Go out of your way to speak with people

Understanding others

On my way to work one morning I could see a rain cloud ahead. I was on my motor bike, and sure enough I caught it and got very wet. I soon passed through it and my bike suit started to dry.

A few miles on, I came to an entrance of a building site where muddy water was pouring across the road. It went up my bike suit and over the front of the bike. It was then back to brilliant sunshine and arriving at work; my boss commented on the good weather. I smiled, thinking to myself "You don't know what I've just been through".

This is true with each other. We all have those experiences when we have made a comment to someone, which is genuine, but we wouldn't have made it, if we knew about the situation the person was going through.

We can't always help those times, but it serves as a reminder that as we speak and meet people in our daily living, we won't know what they either have, or are going through.

At times we will never know, because some people want to keep things to themselves. We hide behind our masks and think we can deal with issues on our own, as it may look like weakness if we ask for help.

Jesus knows and understands everything we are going through as He took our infirmities and carried our sorrows. (Isaiah 53:4) so we can come to Him in our difficulties.

We are also told to "Carry each other's burdens, and in this way you will fulfil the law of Christ". (Galatians 6:2)

True value

I recently went into a well known High Street fashion store and found myself a SALE tee shirt. I saw the original price of £15, but a stick-on red sale ticket was now pricing it at £5, which made it a bargain not to be missed.

On getting it home, I realised that under the £5 sticker there was another stating; now £8, and under that another saying; now £10.

Without going into marketing and retail policy – it left me thinking "What is the real value of the shirt?" I had bought, and how much profit (if any) was made on it.

We all like to get a good deal, knowing that we've got something of value for the least cost.

We also like to be valued ourselves – it is part of our emotional well being, and that is why God speaks to us in His Word about how valuable we are to Him.

Jesus said "Look at the birds of the air, they do not sow or reap or store away in barns, and yet your heavenly Father feeds them. Are you not much more valuable than they?"(Matthew 6:26)

Each of us is valuable in God's sight. He made us, and knows us through and through.

The Message Bible says, "What's the price of a pet canary? Some loose change, right? And God cares what happens to it even more than you do.

He pays even greater attention to you, down to the last detail – even numbering the hairs on your head! So don't be intimidated by all this bully talk. You're worth more than a million canaries. (Read Matthew 10:28-31)

You are valuable in God's sight

Acting on what we hear

For many years in late spring we have seen a bat visit our garden at sunset. Watching this creature is amazing as it makes fast sweeps and turns, flying up to the house windows but never crashing into them.

Despite the old saying as blind as a bat, bats actually have fairly good eyesight; however they use a type of radar to locate objects. For this to work they need good hearing. It's not surprising that bats are capable of hearing a higher sound frequency than any other mammal.

Just as a bat acts quickly and accurately to what they hear back (via their echo/radar system) we can learn a lesson too.

Jesus said "I will show you what he is like who comes to me and hears my words and puts them into practice. He is like a man building a house, who dug down deep and laid the foundation on rock. When a flood came, the torrent struck that house but could not shake it, because it was well-built.

But the one who hears my words and does not put them into practice is like a man who built a house on the ground without a foundation. The moment the torrent struck that house, it collapsed and its destruction was complete". (Luke 7:47-49)

Like the bat that acts and responds to what they hear, we will do well to learn that we need to act in obedience to what we read and hear from the Word of God (the Bible). It is for our blessing and benefit.

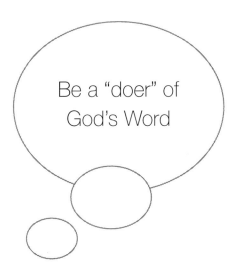

Be a "doer" of God's Word

Building for the best

The day had come to start the building work on putting an additional bedroom into the roof space of our home. Soon, walls were being knocked away, roof tiles had to come off, decoration was being chipped in places and dust was everywhere. I thought back to its original state of being weather proof and nicely decorated and tidy.

To get perspective I had to look towards what it would be like when finished. We would have a superb sea view and extra space.

It is easy to hold onto things in life that give us security, but the lesson here was that we are going to have to experience times of disruption and change, to allow for new and better things to take place.

God is the Architect of our lives. We are not the Building Foreman of our own lives – God is. Follow His instructions because He has a great plan and purpose for your life.

The Christian life can be likened to a building site, where God reveals things in our lives which are wrong or ineffective and that need to be demolished to allow the Lord to rebuild within us, His good and fruitful ways.

In Ephesians 2:19-22 – Paul reminds God's people (members of God's household) that they are built on the foundation of the apostles and prophets, with Christ Jesus himself as the Chief Cornerstone.

In Him the whole building is joined together and rises to become a holy temple in the Lord. And in Him you too are being built together to become a dwelling in which God lives by His Spirit.

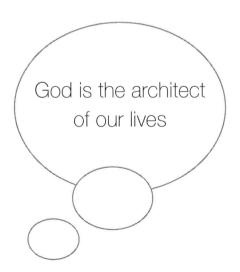

God is the architect of our lives

An anchor in the storm

I have a wonderful sea view from my office window which allows me to see many ships come and go.

For several weeks a large container ship had taken up residence, and I noted how depending on the tide; it faced various directions.

Even though the ship turned, it was firmly anchored and therefore would not end up grounding on the local beach.

An anchor prevents a ship from drifting away due to water currents or tide.

On an anchoring run, a ship would lay the anchor together with a length of its iron cables on the seabed. It is not the weight of the anchor, but the weight of the huge iron cables connected to the anchor that secures the ship. The anchor's weight does play a role, but it is mainly used to grip or hook the iron cables to the seabed.

In the book of Hebrews we are reminded of the hope that God offers to us. We have this hope as an anchor for the soul, firm and secure. (Hebrews 6:19a)

If you are going through one of life's storms at the moment, be encouraged that your hope lies in the promises of God, which act as your anchor.

Many things can come against you, but by trusting in God's promises you can rest secure in Him.

Like the large Container ship, we may still turn in the strong currents and tide, but we will not drift away.

As Priscilla Jane Owens wrote, "We have an anchor that keeps the soul, steadfast and sure while the billows roll; fastened to the rock which cannot move, grounded firm and deep in the Saviour's love".

God's promises
are an anchor
for our lives

Valentine's Day

Some years ago, I was just about to write a Valentine's card to my wife when I noticed that it was the identical one that I had given to her the year before. I must have chosen it again, because the words expressed perfectly my love for her.

I read that in 2012 – £880 million pounds was spent for Valentine's Day (and most of that by men) with the top four gifts being flowers, chocolates, romantic meals and perfume.

The Bible speaks much about the subject of love and types of love. Space does not permit to explain the different aspects of love – but when I say "I love chocolate" – it is not the same kind of love that I feel when I say to my wife "I love you."

The type of love that God wants us to have for one another is a love that cares, and is shown by us giving others our attention and action with loving deeds.

In 1 John 4:7,9 we read "Dear friends, let us love one another, for love comes from God … this is how God showed His love among us: He sent His one and only Son into the world that we might live through Him.

The well known Bible reading from 1 Corinthians 13 is always a good reminder of how we should love others. The Message Bible puts it like this.

Love never gives up. Love cares more for others than for self. Love doesn't want what it doesn't have. Love doesn't strut, doesn't have a swelled head, doesn't force itself on others, isn't always "me first", doesn't fly off the handle, doesn't keep score of the sins of others, doesn't revel when others grovel, takes pleasure in the flowering of truth, puts up with anything, trusts God always, always looks for the best, never looks back, but keeps going to the end. Love never dies.

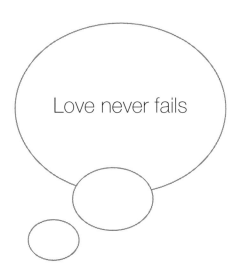

Love never fails

Asteroids

On February 15th 2013 – an asteroid (the size of an Olympic swimming pool) passed by – just 17,200 miles above the Earth. It was travelling at a speed of 17,400 mph! It was noted at the time, "This is a record predicted close approach for an object this size."

Asteroids are small Solar System bodies that orbit the Sun. The Asteroid belt lies roughly between the orbits of Mars and Jupiter in the Solar System and is divided into an inner and outer belt. The inner belt is made of asteroids that are within 250 million miles of the Sun and made of metal. The outer belt includes asteroids 250 million miles beyond the Sun and consists of rocky asteroids.

Today, it is good that we know so much about the universe, yet our knowledge is so small compared with what is still unknown. What is even more amazing is that God, who put it all into place – knows everything about what He has made!

The writer of the book of Hebrews in the Bible reminds us "that the Universe was formed at God's command." The Psalmist wrote concerning God – "The heavens are yours, and yours also the earth; you founded the world and all that is in it." (Psalm 89:11)

While Job was going through his testing times, God asked him some big questions about the Universe.

"Where were you when I laid the earth's foundation .. who marked off its dimensions? ...Can you bring forth the constellations in their seasons? ... Do you know the laws of the heavens?" (Read Job chapter 38)

Job was being reminded that this is God's Universe and He sustains it by His power and wisdom.

Just as God knows all about His universe (including, sun, moon, stars and asteroids!) – He also knows all about us and is interested in every aspect of our lives.

This week; in any problem, anxiousness or decision that you face – remember that the God who made and sustains the Universe, is the One who is able to help and strengthen you. He is only a prayer away.

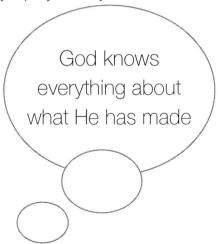

God knows everything about what He has made

Keeping the weeds down

Behind our garden pond many weeds have sprung up over the years.

Some start to creep up through the loose rocks around the edge and others have grown through the protective netting we have had to place over the pond to protect the goldfish from seagull and cat attacks!

To save us time on constant weeding, we decided to go for the option of laying mesh matting over the soil and covering it with small stones.

The matting keeps the light from the soil and this helps keep the weeds down.

The Bible says a lot about weeds. (Matthew 13:24-30, 36-43) In Matthew 13:1-9, Jesus spoke about a farmer who went out to sow his seed. Some of the seed fell among thorns, which grew up and choked the plants.

We need to watch out for the weeds that can easily grow into our lives. In Mark 4:19 we are given more detail. The worries of this life, the deceitfulness of wealth and the desires for other things come in and choke the word, making it unfruitful.

When we believe and act on what we read in God's word we will lead fruitful and effective lives for Him.

Take some time to see if any weeds of worry or wrong desires have started to grow and choke your walk of faith in the Lord.

Should you discover any – talk to God about it. He will help you root out those things that prevent you from experiencing the fullness of His joy and purpose for your life.

God wants us to experience the fullness of His joy

Let go and let God.

A virus alert came up on my home computer screen. Each time I ran a scan I had a reminder of the potential threats that had entered my computer. A Trojan horse was on the loose!

I have no expertise on these things, so I contacted my friend who sorts the system for me.

I thought I would have to take the computer to him to have this virus problem fixed, but as I spoke on the phone he told me what to do to allow him to take over operation of my system from his home.

It was amazing to see him work around the various screens and programmes that I had never seen (and didn't know existed) and then finally applying a "fix" programme.

The Trojan horse was finally in the virus vault and my computer safe again.

In everyday life we can have many threats that come against us, making us lose our peace and joy, and like a virus they can worm their way into us, making us unfruitful and ineffective.

It is good to know that God is interested in all of our problems. Just as I needed to hand control of my computer over to my friend, so we need to hand over all those things to God that we struggle with.

He is the expert in knowing how to deal with every issue that we will ever face.

God is the one who can handle what we can't, so we need to learn to let go and let God direct and keep our lives.

1 Peter 5:7 reminds us to "Cast all your anxiety on Him because He cares for you".

Hand over to God all the things you struggle with

Free inside

Some years ago I was collecting models of a certain "tiger family" that were free inside cornflake packets.

One morning as I opened a new packet, I was digging deep for the model, but soon realised there wasn't one inside.

I felt disappointed as I read the front of the box – "*Free Inside* this packet; one of Tony's friends".

The promise on the packet had not been honoured.

There are many other things in life that can bring hurt, distrust and disappointment to us through broken promises.

A retailer may not keep the promise of a deal or fulfil a guarantee as we expected. Things we say we will do for friends, we may overlook in the busy-ness of our days.

In the Bible God has made many promises.

We can be certain that He will always keep them. His word will not disappoint you or let you down. What He says He will do.

Psalm 145:13b – The Lord is faithful to all his promises... If you are going through a difficult time at present, open the Bible and remind yourself of all that God wants to do in your life.

The prayer of the psalmist in Psalm 119:49-50 is "Remember your word to your servant, for You have given me hope. My comfort in my suffering is this: Your promise renews my life"

May God enable us to keep the promises we make, and may we each know the comfort, peace and hope from all that the LORD promises to us.

God keeps
all of His promises

Be still and know

We live in a culture where we get use to having the radio or TV on – the sound of music or conversation constantly in the background.

From my experiences as an Exam Invigilator, I am aware of the quiet atmosphere that we try to create when students are sitting their GCSE's. I recall a student asking to be moved as the sound of a pigeon in the heating duct above their desk was distracting them.

Another asked me to close windows as the noise was really annoying them. (Not sure if the annoying noise was the flapping blinds from the breeze or the shouting of students from the sports court outside).

When it comes to seeking God in prayer, we need to find a quiet place so we can hear God speak to our hearts and minds. Isaiah 30:15b says" in quietness and trust is your strength."

Jesus and his disciples were experiencing a busy time with people coming and going – they didn't have a chance to eat. Jesus said "Come with me by yourselves to a quiet place and get some rest". (Mark 6:31)

"Be still before the Lord and wait patiently for Him".. (Psalm 37:7a) and "Be still and know that I am God". (Psalm 46:10a)

God does hear our short arrow-type prayers wherever we are and whatever we're doing, but it is vital we make a special time and find that quiet place to pray and hear the still small voice of God speak to us.

In quietness – even before praying a word, we can experience the presence of God, and know He is with us and for us.

Make some time to seek God in quietness

Bird table

When I first moved to Devon, my Mum asked if I would make a bird table for the garden. This I did, and within a couple of hours it was sited on the fence and bread was placed on it in anticipation for the first visitor.

Day by day I looked out of the window to see if any birds were feeding on it, but nothing happened for many weeks.

Then one morning when looking out, I spotted a bird on my table. Not a sparrow, robin or blackbird as I was hoping for, but a large black crow, which was far too big for the construction and taking all the food.

I was happy. I didn't care now what the bird was, because at last my bird table was being used for the purpose I had made it.

God has a plan and a purpose for each one of us – which we can discover as we seek Him through prayer and reading the Bible. Jesus tells us; there is much rejoicing in heaven over one sinner who repents… (Luke 15:7a)

God rejoices when we turn to Jesus His Son and start living according to how God made us to live in following and obeying His ways.

Philippians 2:13 reminds us "for it is God who works in you to will and to act according to his good purpose."

David the Psalmist wrote "The Lord will fulfil his purpose for me….. (Psalm 138:8a)

Proverbs reminds us that seeking God's purpose is the best way. "Many are the plans in a man's heart, but it is the Lord's purpose that prevails". (Proverbs 19:21)

God has a plan and purpose for everyone

Walking in the light

I was recovering from what my doctor had described as some virus. After two weeks, I still tired quickly and the cough lingered.

Searching on the internet I discovered that once viruses are in the body they are quite tough to kill, and antibiotics are powerless against them.

I went on to read that a study at a University in Arizona has shown that something viruses are exposed to all the time (visible light) can be used to kill them.

A strong blast of visible light from a low-power laser can kill viruses. The laser which shines for 100 femtoseconds (one millionth of a billionth of a second!) causes the virus's outer shell to vibrate and become damaged and deactivated while the area around the virus remains unharmed.

The Bible also speaks of the importance of light bringing healing and wholeness into our lives. Our human nature is like a deadly virus – causing us to sin, with the side effects of guilt, shame, pain, brokenness and separation from God.

The Good News is that God's light shines in the darkness (John 1:5a)

Jesus said "Whoever lives by the truth comes into the light.." (John 3:21a) and "I have come into the world as a light, so that no-one who believes in me should stay in darkness". (John 12:46)

In 1 John 1:7 we read "But if we walk in the light as He is in the light, we have fellowship with one another, and the blood of Jesus, His Son, purifies us from every sin." May we live life to the full in the glorious light that Jesus gives.

God's light shines in the darkness

The Power of God

I was half way through cleaning the Art block at the College where I work, when there was a power cut. We still had electricity downstairs, but the upstairs was in darkness. I made the most of the daylight remaining to work in the rooms affected by the cut in supply.

Whenever the electric goes off, we realise just how much we rely on power for everyday living and we can't be as effective trying to work in the darkness.

At Easter time we remind ourselves of the power of God, and His promise that He will empower us to live in His victory, whatever we are going through.

On the Cross; Jesus died to pay the price for our sinfulness. The Apostle Paul tells us that the message of the Cross is foolishness to those who don't believe, but to those who do – it is the power of God. (1 Cor 1:18)

After three days, Jesus rose from the grave. God by His power raised the Lord from the dead, and He will raise us also. (1 Cor 6:14)

God wants each of us to experience His power that transforms our lives and accomplishes His greater purpose in every circumstance.

Peter tells us "God's divine power has given us everything we need for life and godliness" (2 Peter 1:3a)

During the power cut at the College, I was working with limited power. This reminded me of our need to seek the fullness of God's power, purity and presence in all our ways – all of the time.

Take time to gaze afresh upon the power of God. As we read and take God at His word, we will experience His power in our lives.

The message of the Cross of Christ – is the power of God

Pruning

I am not an expert gardener, and when it comes to the task of pruning; it gets done when I have time rather than at the right or best time for the plant.

I was cutting back a shrub in our front garden. (I don't know the type, and it was still in flower!). I had to use some steps as it had grown to about 8 foot high.

I recalled when we planted it out from a pot, many years ago, and it would have been about 18 inches in height. I realised this shrub had grown well, and by pruning on a regular basis, new branches were being established.

Jesus spoke about this aspect of cutting back in reference to our living.

He referred to God, (His Father) as being the Gardener, who cuts off every branch that bears no fruit, while every branch that does bear fruit, is trimmed clean so that it will be even more fruitful. (John 15:1-2)

The unfruitful branches spoken of here refer to our bad habits and sins which God wants to cut away. If we confess our sins to Jesus, He is faithful and just and will forgive us our sins and purify us from all unrighteousness. (1 John 1:9)

God also trims clean, fruitful branches, so that we can bear more fruit. This is not an easy process, but the end result is best for us.

James 1:2 reminds us "Consider it pure joy … whenever you face trials of many kinds, because you know that the testing of your faith develops perseverance.

Perseverance must finish its work so that you may be mature and complete not lacking anything".

We are to be both faithful to God – and fruitful for Him

When troubles come

We have a rain gauge in our garden, and after a prolonged and heavy downpour, noted 1:8 inches of rainwater had fallen. (nearly filling the gauge)

Apart from the obvious problem of flooding that arises from too much rain falling, I noticed something else. Following the rain, we had a period of sunshine that quickly dried up the soil, but also caused it to crack.

We all talk about the weather (it's usually too hot or too cold) and we often refer to troubles in life as "storms."

Jesus referred to the weather speaking in Matthew 7:25 when He said concerning a wise man who had built his house on the rock – "The rain came down, the streams rose, and the winds blow and beat against that house; yet it did not fall, because it had its foundation on the rock".

Where is your confidence, trust and assurance when the hard storms of life beat against you?

No one is exempt from them. Jesus said "In this world you will have trouble. But take heart! I have overcome the world". (John 16:33b)

Psalm 107:28-29 reads "Then they cried out to the Lord in their trouble, and He brought them out of their distress.

He stilled the storm to a whisper; the waves of the sea were hushed".

Are you in the middle of riding out a storm? Call upon the LORD – our Rock and Rescuer.

Take heart – God is with us in our troubles

It's good to talk

I had gone into town to do some shopping. I noticed ahead of me a lady standing outside a shop who appeared to be looking intently at something on the pavement. As I got nearer I realised she was on her mobile phone and she was just glancing down as she concentrated on her call.

As I walked up the steps to home, I paused at the top, and saw a lady behind me – walking and also talking on her mobile. I looked ahead and noticed a young lady – again with a mobile attached to her ear.

We certainly live in a culture of conversation, but not necessarily one of good and positive communication. I've frequently heard people shouting and arguing on their mobiles and thought their call would not be encouraging the receiver. That said – the slogan, "It's good talk" is true. It's great to be able to keep in touch with friends and family and encourage them – even when we are miles apart.

One of the greatest privileges we have is that we can talk with God and ask of him through prayer.

The Psalmist wrote, "I love the Lord, for He heard my voice; He heard my cry for mercy. Because he turned his ear to me, I will call on him as long as I live" {Psalm 116:1-2} It may be a short prayer to God when we initially face problems – "In my distress I called to the Lord... (Psalm 18:6)

At other times we need to take time and be quiet before God (like Jesus did) so that we can talk to Him as well as listen to what He wants to say to us. Mark 6:46 tells us that Jesus left the crowd and went into the hills to pray.

Whatever you are going through today: are you talking to God about it? He's interested and cares about every aspect of your life.

God is waiting
to listen to our
prayers

Peace of mind

We decided that it was time to treat ourselves to a new cooker. (The old one had served us for nearly 28 years!)

As soon as we had agreed to purchase; the saleslady went straight into explaining about the after sales insurance that was available for either three or five years.

For an extra payment, we could have peace of mind, should the cooker break down after the initial guarantee.

In the same week, I also had a phone call from our car insurers offering us cover for personal injury – should we be involved in an accident. For 40p a week, I could again purchase that peace of mind.

There is now insurance available for most things, including private health, weddings, travel, residential care for the future and credit payment cover.... but what do we do about our day to day worries and concerns when we are faced with difficult decisions, disappointment, heartache and brokenness?

Insurance can't help here – but Jesus can. He said "Peace I leave with you, my peace I give you. I do not give to you as the world gives. Do not let your hearts be troubled and do not be afraid." (John 14:27)

Paul wrote, "Do not be anxious about anything, but in everything, by prayer and petition, with thanksgiving, present your requests to God.

And the peace of God, which transcends all understanding, will guard your hearts and minds in Christ Jesus". (Philippians 4:6-7)

God is our assurance and confidence at all times and in all situations.

The peace that God gives is beyond our understanding

The seagull

I looked out of my window and noticed a young seagull was standing on the netting of my garden pond – pecking away. I assumed he was after my goldfish for breakfast.

I ran out to chase the gull away, but instead of taking off, it just swiftly walked to the end of the garden and tried to hind behind a pot. Realising it was a young gull that couldn't yet fly, (and there did not seem to be a parent gull hanging around) I left it alone and provisionally made some phone calls as to what to do with a gull that wouldn't move from your garden.

An hour and a half later it was still there, but had gone to the other side of the garden by some tiles. As I walked towards the gull, it started to waddle along the path. I gave chase …it continued up the path and I was able to channel it through a small gap between the garage and house.

Running through the house I caught up with the gull again as it walked out into the road. By this time I was beginning to feel guilty that it may get hit by a car, or cause a problem for traffic on the bend in the road it was now approaching.

I continued to watch the young gull as it finally walked into a safe area away from the road.

That incident reminded me of two things that God wants us to understand as we walk by faith as His disciples.

Just as I was watching the gull to know it was safe, God is watching over us every moment of each day. We may feel we're walking a lonely road at times, but God promises that He will be with us, and will never leave or forsake us.(Deut 31:6)

Secondly – the seagull was at its stage in life when the parent gulls are teaching their young to fly. As followers of Jesus Christ – God wants to us to soar (mount to great heights) in our faith, as we trust in His goodness.

What crisis, challenge or decision faces you right now? As you pray for God's help and wisdom, may He encourage you in your life journey, so that you are sure of what you hope for, and certain of what you don't see. (Hebrews 11:1) That's faith!

God is watching over you every moment of the day

Street corner

I was waiting to cross a road. It was on a ninety degree bend.

From where I was standing I could see what traffic was coming from each direction, but obviously the cars approaching the bend were not able to see if there was anything coming.

As with any sharp bend in the road, they have to be approached with caution as we don't know the position or size of any vehicle that may be heading towards us.

Life at times can seem like a sharp blind bend to us. We don't know what lies ahead round the next corner. There is a quote that says "Don't fear tomorrow. God is already there."

God stands at the corner of our lives and wants us to trust Him in all our ways.

The psalmist wrote "The Lord will watch over your coming and going both now and for evermore." (Psalm 121: 8)

What decisions do you face at this time? King Solomon wrote in Proverbs "In all your ways acknowledge the Lord, and He will make your paths straight."

The sharp bends on life's road will come to us all but the Bible tells us that God … will be our guide even to the end." (Psalm 48:14)

The Lord will watch over your coming and going

Be thankful

I had just made a small purchase from a High Street store. On checking my change, I noticed the person at the till had given me £1 extra change.

I waited until the customer after me had been served; and then went back and explained they had given me too much change, and handed the one pound coin back.

This immediately caused confusion, as the assistant struggled about the procedure required to put the till correct.

In working this through, it distracted them from thanking me for my honesty.

In the gospel of Luke (17:11-19) Jesus spoke of ten lepers who were all healed but only one came back to thank him.

The Psalmist in the Bible encourages us to give thanks to the Lord for He is good... I will give thanks, for you answered me. (Psalm 118:21)

It has been said that we need to develop an attitude of gratitude.

When we thank others for who they are and the things they do, they will feel valued and appreciated.

It has been said that "Silent gratitude isn't very much use to anyone." May we express our thanks this week to God and to others.

Develop an attitude of gratitude

Time watching

One of my jobs is being an Exam Invigilator. When an exam commences the start and finish time is immediately put up on the board for everyone to see, so the students can gauge if they are managing their time in answering all questions adequately to gain maximum marks.

In certain exams, some students finish early and in others they are writing up to the last minute.

While invigilating, I find myself looking at the clock or my watch very frequently and time appears to pass very slowly.

In between responding to student's requests; I try to use that time wisely and keep my mind active, by praying for the students or thinking through things I need to plan and prepare for.

The use and management of our time is an important issue for all of us. The Bible tells us in Ecclesiastes 3:1, "There is a time for everything, and a season for every activity under heaven." Solomon went on to say "the wise heart will know the proper time and procedure."

In my preaching file I keep this reflection: Each day, we are credited with 86,400 seconds. Every night it writes off, as lost, whatever of this you have failed to invest to good purpose.

To realise the value of one year, ask a student who failed an exam. To realise the value of one week, ask the editor of a weekly newspaper. To realise the value of one minute ask the person who missed the train.

David the Psalmist wrote, "…I trust in you O Lord; I say, You are my God. My times are in your hands"

There is a time for everything…

Lost confidence

I really enjoy playing the guitar, and for several years, I thought I would like to treat myself to an Electro Classical guitar. (That's a nylon string – Spanish sounding guitar that you can plug in direct to amplify)

When funds allowed, I went to view various models and after trying out several in the shop, made a purchase. Over the next week I kept picking up the guitar at various times throughout the day and started playing.

I noticed there was a buzzing sound on several strings and frets. I restrung it, but that did not resolve the problem.

I returned it to the Retailer and they very kindly offered help to rectify it – but my experience had made me lose confidence in that style of guitar and I asked if I could exchange it for an Electric model that I was more familiar with. My request was granted.

Losing confidence in a product is minor compared to circumstances in life that shake or make us lose our confidence. You may have been turned down at a job interview, failed an exam or made a costly mistake …

When we trust God in these situations, the Bible tells us that "the Lord will be your confidence." (Proverbs 3:26)

God also wants us to be confident in coming to him.

The apostle Paul wrote; "In Jesus Christ – and through faith in him, we may approach God with freedom and confidence." (Ephesians 3:12)

So we can say with confidence, the Lord is my helper; I will not be afraid. (Hebrews 13:6)

The Lord will be your confidence

A lamp to our feet

We were visiting some friends who lived out in "the sticks." We had to park the car a few hundred metres away from their house and walk up a path.

When it came to leaving, a heavy mist had descended in the area. Our friends offered us the use of a lamp, but we said no – it was OK, as the path back to the car was reasonably even and straight.

We hadn't walked far from their house lights, when we realised we would need the lamp as we couldn't see the way ahead at all. We went back for the lamp and got safely back to the car.

God's word; the Bible, is a light for our lives. Like us initially, (when we thought we could make our short journey without the lamp) – many try to navigate through life without a light.

The Psalmist writes "Your word is a lamp to my feet and a light to my path." (Psalm 119:105)

With the lamp we borrowed I could shine it near our feet to keep us from tripping, but also shine it on the path ahead to ensure we were heading in the right direction.

Are you needing some direction right now, or some light on a darkened path?

As we trust God's Word, He will guard and guide our steps. Jesus said "I am the light of the world. Whoever follows me will never walk in darkness, but will have the light of life." (John 8:12)

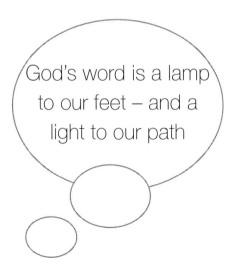

God's word is a lamp to our feet – and a light to our path

Wimbledon Tennis

The month of June sees the start of the Lawn Tennis Championship at Wimbledon. Thousands of spectators come through the famous SW19 gates every year to watch the very best talents in world tennis.

I very much enjoy Wimbledon (even though it's only watching from our lounge sofa) I've played a little tennis myself in the past – but most of the exercise came from collecting the balls after they had veered off my racket and gone way out of court!

A television advert for Wimbledon Tennis showed many well known players – with varied facial expressions showing determination, concentration, and jubilation. The short clip concluded with the words – "It only hurts so much – because they want it so bad."

I read that Tennis players must practice the way they want to play. If they only practice at 50% intensity, they will find it hard to get into the higher gear needed for the real match. The effort and commitment required is huge for every single shot they hit.

The Bible has much to say about determined effort and is a training manual for our lives. Someone once commented that B.I.B.L.E stands for Basic Information Before Leaving Earth!

The apostle Paul said "Train yourself to be godly." He went onto acknowledge that ".. physical training is of some value, but godliness has value for all things, holding promise for both the present life and the life to come." (1 Timothy 4:7-8)

The writer of the book of Hebrews points out what we should put our effort into. "Make every effort to live in peace with all men and to be holy …" (Hebrews 12:14)

When we trust in, and live by God's promises we participate in the life that God has in store for us.

Just as a Wimbledon Champion will put their effort and time into working on their strength, flexibility, stamina, speed and agility – may it remind us that we should make every effort to add the following to our faith: good character, spiritual understanding, alert discipline, passionate patience, reverent wonder, warm friendliness and generous love. (2 Peter 1:5-7 – The Message Bible)

We need to make every effort – to keep building on our faith

Cannon ball

We were having our garage rebuilt: and during the time when clearing out, we found what we thought was a small cannon ball.

A few days later I was talking to the builder about it, and he advised me that it was a drain ball. I had to ask what a drain ball was used for!

I was told that this heavy ball, would have been used to roll down drains – to ensure that all the joints on the pipes were clear of sand and cement and also smooth, to allow the water and sewerage to drain away freely.

It was good to know the truth about this and learn some facts about a drain ball, although I was a little disappointed, thinking what I thought was a cannon ball may have been linked to the near-by historic Napoleonic fort at Berry Head.

Discovering truth brings us into contact with reality and reveals the importance of accuracy. The Bible has much to say about truth.

David the Psalmist said of God "Behold, You desire truth in the inner being…" (Psalm 51:6) David went on to proclaim "Teach me your way, O Lord, and I will walk in your truth… (Psalm 86:11)

Whatever decision, circumstance or difficulty you may be experiencing this week – God's Word of truth can help and guide you.

The Bible tells us about the Good News of God's plan and purpose for our lives. Not only is God's Word true, but He is The Truth. In John's gospel, Jesus said to those who believed Him, "…you will know the truth, and the truth will set you free." (John 8:32)

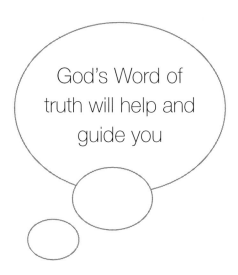

God's Word of truth will help and guide you

Rainbows

From my office window I have taken many photographs of rainbows over Torbay. Over the years there have been some very vivid ones, but also several double bows.

I discovered that in double rainbows, the second arc seen outside the primary arc, has the order of its colours reversed – red facing toward the other one in both rainbows.

The second bow is caused by light reflecting twice inside water droplets.

God first placed a rainbow in the sky as a sign of His covenant with Noah. (You can read the full story in the Bible in Genesis 9:1-17)

God told Noah that each time he saw a rainbow in the clouds, he could be assured that God was remembering His promise.

In this book – I have shared about other promises from God that can be found in the Bible – His promises of help, guidance, peace, fulfilment, strength and forgiveness …as we trust God and take Him at His word.

The best visibility condition for a rainbow is when there is a dark cloud behind it.

If you are experiencing a dark cloud of crisis in your life at present, remember that as the sun is always behind you when you face a rainbow, God is always there when you call upon and trust in Him.

The Psalmist wrote "I call on the Lord in my distress, and He answers me." (Psalm 120:1)

Rainbows remind us that God keeps His Word

Names

My name is James but I've always preferred being called Jim (and it's not because James means supplanter!)

I was thinking recently about the names of my family. There is a Jim Collins who writes books and is a well known Business Consultant.

I have a brother named Michael. (Michael Collins was a former American Astronaut whose second space flight was as Command Module Pilot for Apollo 11.) My Dad was called Phil. (the same name as the famous Phil Collins, singer/songwriter, drummer, pianist and actor)

We may have the same name as these people, but we can't claim to have done the things they are known for. Each one of us have been created by God, and He has plans for our lives that will give us a hope and a future, if we follow and trust Him. The most important thing in life, is how we live it out before God and others.

King Solomon wrote "A good name is more desirable than great riches ...and better than fine perfume." (Proverbs 22:1/Ecclesiastes 7:1)

God knows His creation by name. "He who brings out the starry host one by one, and calls them each by name. Because of His great power and mighty strength, not one of them is missing." (Isaiah 40:26)

When Moses was leading God's people, Moses asked that God's Presence went with them.

God answered Moses, "I will do the very thing you have asked, because I am pleased with you and I know you by name."

God knows everything about each of us and knows our names. He wants us to know Him by name.

The Psalmist wrote "Those who know your Name will trust in you, for you LORD, have never forsaken those who seek you." (Psalm 9:10)

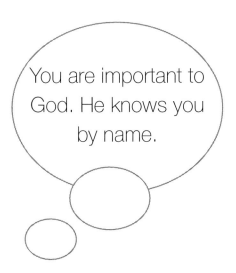

You are important to God. He knows you by name.

Watch where you walk!

While we were having our garage rebuilt it was discovered that we would need some additional concrete work to be carried out. The garage base needed to be thicker, and half the drive had to be re-laid with a small gradient to allow for rain water to drain away.

It is during those times when cement is drying you have to remember to watch where you walk, and take precautions to keep animals away.

It wasn't until a few weeks later that one of the builders pointed out to me a single paw print in the cement. A neighbourhood cat had made its lasting impression on our drive!

It reminded me of a saying that a family member had put in my autograph book when I was younger. "The future lies before you, like a sheet of driven snow. Be careful how you tread it, as every step will show."

King Solomon wrote "a prudent man gives thought to his steps." (Proverbs 14:15) Every day each of us will be making and leaving an impression on others by our words and deeds.

Paul the apostle said, "Be very careful, then, how you live – not as unwise but as wise" .. (Ephesians 5:15)

Again, Paul writing to the Galatians speaks of nine qualities that God wants us to experience in our lives and be evident to others …love, joy, peace, patience, kindness, goodness, faithfulness, gentleness and self control. (Galatians 5:22-23) May these characteristics be our lasting impression.

We need to give thought to our steps

Heart condition

I received a letter, and on the envelope it read "What is the state of the Nation's heart health?" It gave me a chance to get involved in the nation's biggest-ever heart survey. I completed the form and returned it.

The human heart is an amazing organ. The size of an adult heart is about the size of two fists and beats 100,000 times a day which is 35 million times a year.

In an average lifetime a heart will beat around 3 billion times and pump 1 million barrels of blood around the body (which is enough to fill more than 3 Super-tankers)

The heart beat is life to us – so it's not surprising that we are told to look after our heart by healthy eating and lifestyle choices and regular exercise.

The Bible speaks much about the human heart. King Solomon wrote "Above all else, guard your heart, for it is the wellspring of life". "As water reflects a face, so a man's heart reflects the man." (Proverbs 4:23 /27:19)

Jesus taught us about the attitudes that we should hold in our hearts."Do not store up treasures on earth, but store up for yourselves treasures in heaven. For where your treasure is, there your heart will be also." (Matthew 6:21)

Jesus later explained to his disciples "the things that come out of the mouth come from the heart" (We can soon discover what is on a person's heart, if we just listen to them)

As we answer that survey question personally; "What is the state of our heart health." – when our trust is in God; we can reply like the Psalmist, "My flesh and my heart may fail, but God is the strength of my heart and my portion forever." (Psalm 73:26)

Our heart is where our treasure is. May God be our greatest treasure.

The need for change

We had just had our new cooker delivered. It had all the up to date features, and the colour and size was perfect.

One of the main things we were looking forward to; was to have the automatic timer so we could bring the oven on to cook things while we were away and come back to a cooked meal. This feature had broken on our old one and would not have been worth repairing.

We soon discovered that our new cooker timer was faulty and the timer had to be replaced. This worked for a couple of "test" times but broke again the same day. Another timer was fitted.

The Repair technician told me that he had noticed that the timer unit had a few changes to the software and maybe these changes had come as a result of realising the old type was not functioning as it should.

No matter how often the timer was exchanged, it was not going to work until things within had been changed. Jesus spoke about attitudes within us that need to change; when the disciples came and asked him, "Who is the greatest in the kingdom of heaven?"

In Matthew 18:3-4 He replies, "I tell you the truth, unless you change and become as little children, you will never enter the kingdom of heaven.

Therefore, whoever humbles himself like this child is the greatest in the kingdom of heaven".

Little children do not strive for honour and power – they are innocent, humble and trusting. May we each ask God to change us so these qualities are evident in our lives.

We need to change – and become child-like in our trusting

Go bless

I always run a spell-check over my letters and articles I write on the computer, but I also read the documents through again before sending.

On one occasion I found that I had finished an email with the words "Go bless." I meant to write "God bless."

After correcting this spelling error, I realised there was a lesson I could learn from this. "God blesses us, so we can go and bless others".

God is good, and His blessing is about Him bestowing His goodness upon us and creation. The psalmist acknowledged this in writing "May God be gracious to us and bless us and make His face to shine upon us." (Psalm 67:1)

Trusting in God does not make us exempt from problems and suffering in life – but He does promise His grace, favour and strength to those that seek Him. Concerning Jesus, John wrote "From the fullness of His grace we have all received one blessing after another." (John 1:16)

When God blesses us, it is not just for our benefit, but is to enable and encourage us to be a blessing to others. Jesus said "It is more blessed to give than to receive."

In His Sermon on the Mount, Jesus talked about nine attitudes and actions of our heart that will bring us blessing – true joy, happiness and satisfaction. These included being meek, merciful, pure in heart and being peace makers. (Matthew 5:1-12)

We can bless and be blessed in many ways – sending a card or making a phone call just to say you are thinking of someone, or taking a cake or some sweets to a shut-in neighbour.

This week, may we think about and be thankful to God for His blessing upon us, and as we do, may we Go – and bless, bringing some happiness and well being into the lives of others.

It is more blessed to give than to receive

A way with words

I've enjoyed writing since I was about eight years old, and I recall the excitement I felt when I had my first short poem entitled "Christmas" published in the local "Reading Chronicle" (That is Reading – the town in Berkshire and not reading, as in looking at printed words.)

I read recently "Aoccdrnig to rscheearch at an Elingsh uinervtisy, it deosn't mttaer in waht oredr the ltteers in a wrod are, olny taht the frist and lsat ltteres are at the rghit pcleas. Tihs is bcuseae we do not raed ervey lteter by ilstef, but the wrod as a wlohe."

The spacing between words is vital or the meaning of sentences will be completely changed. How do you read "Opportunityisnowhere" It could mean "Opportunity is nowhere" or on a more positive note "Opportunity is now here."

The words we speak each day to those we meet are very important. In the Bible King Solomon wrote many proverbs concerning this matter. "Reckless words pierce like a sword, but the tongue of the wise brings healing. Truthful lips endure forever, but a lying tongue lasts only a moment" (Proverbs 12:19) He went on to say "Pleasant words are a honeycomb, sweet to the soul…"

Kind and encouraging words will always build others up, but criticism and harsh words will tear down.

In addition to watching the words we speak, we also need to be aware of how we speak. "A soft answer turns away wrath, but a harsh word stirs up anger. The tongue of the wise uses knowledge rightly, but the mouth of fools pours forth foolishness." (Proverbs 15:1-2)

In the conversations that we have this coming week, may we heed the words of the apostle Paul who said "Let your conversation be always full of grace, seasoned with salt, so that you may know how to answer everyone." (Colossians 4:6)

Kind words will build others up

To serve or be served

It's always nice when going out for the day to find a Cafe or Shop where we can enjoy a morning coffee or afternoon tea. (and a doughnut or tea-cake!) My wife and I have favourite places in certain local towns which have become our regular refreshment venues while out on our shopping trips.

We may go back to a place because we know and like the menu options – it is in a convenient location or has a scenic view from the window.

On those occasions when we go to a Coffee House or Tea Room for the first time, my first thought is normally "Do we have to go and order?" or "Do we get served?"

Whether we are served at the table or served after ordering – I appreciate the dedication and commitment that staff give when serving customers.

It is a pleasure to be served, but it is also a privilege to serve others. The Bible has much to say about serving.

Jesus said… "the Son of Man did not come to be served, but to serve, and to give his life as a ransom for many." (Mark 10:45) The prophet Isaiah described Jesus as a suffering servant when he wrote – He was .. "a man of sorrows, and familiar with suffering… surely He took up our infirmities and carried our sorrows… He was pierced for our transgressions, the punishment that brought us peace was upon him, and by his wounds we are healed." (Isaiah 53:3-5)

As we experience the blessings of forgiveness, healing, mercy, love and compassion that Jesus offers to us, He calls us to serve Him and others.

The apostle Peter wrote "Each one should use whatever gift he has received to serve others" ... (1 Peter 4:10)

Many of us will remember the British Sitcom TV programme about Grace Brothers (based in the ladies and gentlemen's clothing section of a department store) – with the well known title and main line of "Are you being served?"

As we are served by others this week, may we show and share our appreciation to them – but also consider the question "Who can I serve?"

Paul said to the believers in Ephesus, "Serve wholeheartedly, as if you were serving the Lord, not men."

We are to use the gifts we have to serve others

Fairground ride.

One summer I went to the local fair with some friends. I was encouraged to go on the Noah's Ark. This is quite a timid ride compared to what there is available today – it was a roundabout and the wooden animals you sat on also went up and down. I recall mounting a horse – paid my fare and the ride commenced. After several turns, I found that my knuckles were gripping the handles each side of the horse's head rather tightly, as my body started to lean out to the left. In a panic I thought "I'm not going to be able stay on this horse if it carries on like this – I'm going to get thrown off."

Suddenly – an arm grabbed my shoulder and pulled me in. The young fair ride assistant said "All you have to do is lean in". I continued the ride in safety but often think back to what might have happened if the assistant hadn't noticed I was struggling.

In my preaching, I've frequently referred to my fairground ride to what God did for me. "When I was going my own way – being distant from God, His strong arm came and drew me to Himself."

From cover to cover, the Bible is full of stories of God coming to the rescue of those who trust Him.

The very heart of the gospel is that God sent His Son Jesus to rescue and save us; from the guilt and shame caused by our sinfulness and selfishness, by offering us His forgiveness.

Daniel (who had been falsely accused) was thrown into the Lion's den. As the King gave the order he said to Daniel "May your God, whom you serve continually, rescue you." God came to the rescue in sending an angel to shut the mouths of the lions. (Daniel Chapter 6)

In the Book of Acts, Stephen quotes Joseph's experience. "Because the patriarchs were jealous of Joseph, they sold him as a slave into Egypt. But God rescued him from all his troubles". (Acts 7:9-10)

Are you in need this week of some help and strength for a difficult situation? God still comes to the rescue of those who will follow Him. God Himself declared in Psalm 81:7 – "In your distress you called and I rescued you"

God sent His Son Jesus – to save us

Involve me and I learn

At the College where I work, there is a quote by Benjamin Franklin over the sinks in the Staff toilets. It reads "Tell me and I forget. Teach me and I remember. Involve me and I learn." (Benjamin Franklin was the 6th President of Pennsylvania from 1785-1788 and among many other things he was a leading author, scientist, inventor and musician. I discovered this as I wanted to learn a little more about the man behind the quote)

Having done some guitar teaching – I'm aware that I can explain verbally where fingers go to make chords and even draw diagrams that will help students remember, but unless they have guitar in hand and are involved in attempting to play it – they will not learn.

I am also reminded that Jesus taught and modelled discipleship to His followers. He shared and showed them the way to God, and the way to live life – but also involved His disciples by sending them out to do what He had said and done. (Read Luke 9:1-2)

Jesus could have done many miracles without using anyone else but He longed to be involved in people's lives. The same is still true for us today!

Before the feeding of the 5000 Jesus said to his disciples "You give them something to eat." Jesus involved them to find out what they did have to eat (5 loaves and 2 fish) and also asked them to serve.

They played their part in the miracle by being obedient and giving what was available.

We start our learning by coming to God. Jesus said "Come to me, all you who are weary and burdened, and I will give you rest. Take my yoke upon you and learn from me, for I am gentle and humble in heart, and you will find rest for your souls." (Matthew 11:28-29) The yoke that Jesus speaks of – is one of obedience to His ways.

We can understand much about God from reading the Bible, and build up great knowledge of the scriptures, but to experience God's involvement in our lives – we need to heed what Jesus' brother James said. "Do not merely listen to the word… Do what it says…" (James 1:22) That's learning!

God wants to be
involved in your life

Driftwood

Following a week of stormy weather, I was taking a walk across a local beach. Alongside seaweed (and a host of other plastic objects) that had been washed up – I observed some nice pieces of various sized driftwood.

Driftwood; which is mainly the remains of trees washed into the ocean by flooding and high winds – has some good uses. It can provide shelter and food for birds, fish and other aquatic species, as it floats in the sea.

Shipworms (saltwater clams) and bacteria can decompose driftwood and turn it into nutrients that are introduced to the food web.

Driftwood can become the foundation for sand dunes, and has also become a popular art form, used in making decorative furniture and other artistic structures.

A thought came to me. "If a piece of tree wood could be used in so many helpful ways – how much more does God want to make our lives useful to Him and others!"

The apostle Paul wrote to Timothy saying "All scripture is God-breathed and is useful for teaching, rebuking, correcting and training in righteousness, so that the man of God may be thoroughly equipped for every good work." (2 Timothy 3:16-17)

Driftwood is shaped and directed by tides and winds. As we trust the promises, and obey the commands of scripture – we are shaped and directed by God. He makes us into the people He wants us to be, and to do the things He wants us to do.

Paul reminded the Ephesians that "we are God's workmanship, created in Christ Jesus to do good works, which God prepared in advance for us to do." (Ephesians 2:10)

God wants to use our words, actions, talents, abilities and creativity… to bring honour to Him and be a blessing and help to those we meet in our daily lives.

God wants to use your life to honour Him and bring blessing to others

God's will

My wife and I made a "Will" over 25 years ago and we realised that they needed up-dating. On visiting our Solicitor we discussed and then agreed the changes to our will, and gave direction as to how we would want our property distributed when we die.

This process reminded me that God has a good and perfect will for each of us. When my wife and I amended our Wills, we made the choices that we felt were best.

Discovering God's will for our lives is found in reading and heeding what He asks of us through His Word – the Bible.

David the Psalmist wrote "To do your will, O my God, is my desire" (Psalm 40: 8). He made a choice to do things God's way; which is not always easy – and He asked for God's help.

David prayed "Teach me to do your will for you are my God; may your good Spirit lead me on level ground." (Psalm 143:10)

Jesus said to His disciples, "I have come down from heaven not to do my will – but to do the will of Him (God the Father) who sent me." (John 6:38-40)

Jesus also reinforced how important it is for us, to seek and to know God's will – when He said to His disciples "This is how you should pray …

Our Father in heaven, your kingdom come, your will be done on earth as it is in heaven." (Matthew 6:9-13)

God's will is God's Word – and God's Word is God's will for us. The Bible reveals God's will and direction for every situation that comes our way in life.

A legal Will to distribute a person's estate, has no force while the person is alive and can be altered or revoked at any time. In contrast; God's Will and eternal purpose for us is unchanging in that He wants us to experience the joy and blessing of His perfect will – every day of our lives.

Let us pray that God's will be done on earth as it is in heaven.

Eye test

I had gone to my optician for my regular eye test and to check out a floater that had appeared across the vision of one of my eyes. I had to have the pupils of my eyes dilated so a further examination could be made.

When eyes are examined, it has been likened to looking into a room through a partially open door – you only see a portion of the room.

When pupils are dilated, it is then like a door that is wide open and you can see much more of the room. Dilation of the pupils allows an Optician to be able to see more of the structures inside the eye and detect problems.

The Bible reveals the spiritual importance of seeing and vision. God knows all things, and also sees all things. King David declared "My frame was not hidden from you when I was made in the secret place… your eyes saw my unformed body." (Psalm 139:15-16)

The Message Bible quotes the words of Jesus in Matthew 6:22-23 like this. "Your eyes are windows into your body. If you open your eyes wide in wonder and belief, your body fills up with light."

When we keep our eyes fixed on Jesus, the author and perfector of our faith – He will guide and direct us in every circumstance and decision in our lives.

I read a quote that said – "Eyes that look are common. Eyes that see are rare."

The psalmist had a desire to see – when he prayed "Open my eyes that I may see wonderful things in your law." (Psalm 119:18)

God knows all things and sees all things

Choices

It was my wife's birthday and we were visiting one of our favourite restaurants to celebrate the occasion. We noticed the menus had been reprinted since our last visit and on looking through them, we discovered several new choices available – especially on the desserts page!

Whether we are buying a service or product – shops and businesses certainly give their customers a huge choice to cover variety and personal preference.

When we were walking home after our meal, I noticed a sign in an Ice cream shop window – displaying pictures of the 25 flavours which were available!

Every day; we all have to make decisions and choices - both big and small. It has been said "You are free to choose, but the choices you make today will determine what you will have, be, and do in the tomorrows of your life."

God is an expert in helping us to make good and right choices in every circumstance of our lives. He wants us to choose Him and His ways.

In the Bible; Joshua was encouraging the tribes of Israel to serve God. He told them "Now fear the Lord and serve him with all faithfulness."

He went on to say – "Choose for yourselves this day whom you will serve …but as for me and my household, we will serve the Lord." (Joshua 24:14-15)

Joshua made a decision of his will – to live life God's way.

The Psalmist wrote, "I have chosen the way of truth; I have set my heart on your laws." (Psalm 119:30)

Choosing God's way may be difficult at times – but His way is always the best for each of us. When we are offended by others – God asks us to choose forgiving them. When we meet difficult people – God asks that we choose to be patient with them.

The psalmist went on to ask "May your hand be ready to help me, for I have chosen your precepts." (Psalm 119: 173) God will help us – as we choose to do what He asks of us.

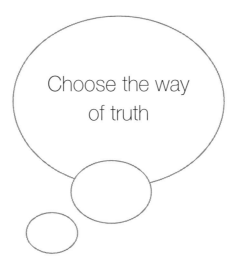

Choose the way
of truth

Snail trail

One autumn morning, I looked out to our conservatory window and noticed that the outside of the glass was covered with dew, and I could not see out. Then I noticed a snail (thankfully; also outside) and could see exactly where it had been, because as it moved, it also took away the dew.

Apparently, a snail only has one foot. It moves with a series of muscular contractions, like waves that pass along the bottom of its foot. To help it move, a snail produces a trail of slime from a gland under its mouth. It is these trails we see on paths, plant pots and on windows.

The snail I observed did not seem to have a purpose in its travels, as I tried to follow its trail; firstly down, then up a bit, then a circle, then?!

Purpose in life for people is vital, and the Bible mentions it many times. God has a plan and purpose for each of us. David the Psalmist wrote "The Lord will fulfil his purpose for me". (Psalm 138:8)

Proverbs tells us that "Many are the plans in a man's heart, but it is the Lord's purpose that prevails". (Proverbs 19:21)

God has a mission and a ministry for each of us to discover and bring glory to Him by fulfilling. It may be hospitality, caring, encouraging...

When Paul, Silas and Timothy wrote to the Church of the Thessalonians their constant prayer for them was "that our God may count you worthy of His calling, and that by His power He may fulfil every good purpose of yours and every act prompted by your faith". (2 Thess 1:11)

May this be our prayer also as we seek to follow God's purposes in all we do.

God has a perfect plan and purpose for your life

Teamwork

It was the start of a new term at the School where I work, and both teaching and support staff attended a training session to look at how we could "build on our success."

At the end of the time we spent together, I understood afresh how my work as a cleaner and exam invigilator was contributing to achieve the vision of the College – because I was "part of the team!"

One definition of teamwork is: the combined action of a group, especially when effective and efficient. Some years ago, I recall seeing a recruitment advertisement for the Royal Navy. The key line read "The Team Works!"

Working together as a team is vital if we are to accomplish our goals. It was during the Olympic Games in 2012, that I realised how individual athletes still needed their coach, training partner and others in their support team. Teamwork is God's idea. He thought of it first and created us to function best when we work together, rather than go it alone.

The apostle Paul used the illustration of a human body to show how God uses teamwork in His Church. He said, "The body is a unit, though it is made up of many parts, and though its parts are many, they form one body." (1 Corinthians 12:12)

The Message Bible goes on to say – "The way God designed our bodies is a model for understanding our lives together as a church: every part dependant on every other part" ...

This week, most of us will have an opportunity where we will experience teamwork, as we involve others in our lives. It may come when we ask family, friends or neighbours for their advice or an opinion – requesting help with a task that we can't manage on our own – or when we offer a listening ear to someone. Teamwork is evident as we give of ourselves to one another and receive from others.

King Solomon wrote in Ecclesiastes 4:9-10, "Two are better than one, because they have a good return for their work: If one falls down, his friend can help him up!"

There is no "I" in teamwork

Achievements

In October 2012, a 43 year old Austrian, Felix Baumgartner became the first Skydiver to go faster than the speed of sound reaching 833.9 miles per hour.

He jumped out of a balloon, 24 miles above New Mexico. Although Felix smashed the record for the highest ever freefall – he almost aborted the dive because his helmet visor fogged up. A great achievement!

Most of us won't be able, (or even want to) achieve things like that – but most of us hope that we will achieve something significant in our life time.

I enjoy playing guitar, singing and song writing – but I don't think I will be getting a song in The Top Ten. However – by giving guitar lessons, I have passed on my skills to a good number of people who are now playing the instrument. Maybe; one of those people will get a song in the charts in the future!

God has made each of us to do works that will be pleasing to Him and of benefit to others.

The Bible reminds us: "the people who know their God shall be strong, and carry out great exploits." (Daniel 11:32)

Everything that God calls us to do will give us purpose and significance. He enables us … "to do good, to be rich in good deeds, and to be generous and willing to share." (1 Timothy 6:18)

Concerning God's Word, the prophet Isaiah wrote "As the rain and the snow come down from heaven, and do not return to it without watering the earth… so is My Word… it will accomplish what I desire and achieve the purpose for which I sent it." (Isaiah 55:10-11)

We can accomplish and achieve God's best and highest purpose for our lives – as we trust in and obey His Words.

The people who know their God shall be strong

Loyalty card

"Have you got a loyalty card?" I'm sure most of us will have been asked this question as we've come to pay for our items in certain Shops.

Having a card with a Store enables us to earn points with the purchases we make – and our loyalty is rewarded as we use the points to pay for our shopping.

A local Radio station was asking listeners to let them know how many loyalty cards they owned. One lady had over 30! A man commented on the difficulty he experienced, trying to find the right card in his wallet at the Checkout. (I don't have that problem – as I only have one card)

Loyalty and faithfulness are important to God. The Psalmist wrote "Blessed is he whose hope is in the Lord his God – who remains faithful forever." (Psalm 146:5-6)

God rewards those who are loyal to Him and obedient to His words. King David said "The ordinances of the Lord are true and righteous altogether .. by them your servant is warned and in keeping them there is great reward." (Psalm 19:9-11)

The writer of the Book of Hebrews reminds us – "without faith it is impossible to please God, because anyone who comes to Him must believe that He exists and that He rewards those who earnestly seek Him." (Hebrews 11:6)

A High Street Store may reward us with a few points for our loyalty; but God's reward to those who seek Him, is that they will find Him – and in God we find forgiveness, love, peace, hope and purpose for life.

Loyalty will involve taking time and effort to maintain meaningful relationships and friendships.

When you use one of your loyalty cards in a shop this week, think about how you could show loyalty to your family, friends and neighbours. It may involve visiting them – when they are in need of some encouragement, or a telephone call to show they are being thought of.

King David prayed for God's people to "keep their hearts loyal to you". (1 Chronicles 29:18) The ever faithful God enables us to be loyal and faithful to Him and others.

Two edged sword

I was walking around Brixham harbour during the Pirate Festival Weekend. One of the many things you could do was "Pick a sword fight" – where you could duel with one of the pirate crew. As I walked along the Quay I found a stall that was selling cutlass swords and scabbards. This was a very authentic pirate weekend!

The duelling and the swords reminded me of the Bible verse in Hebrews 4:12 -"The word of God is living and active. Sharper than any double-edged sword.

A two edged sword has two cutting edges. This was important in a battlefield situation when fighting against multiple opponents at the same time – as it gave the ability to respond quickly from many directions. Swords were not just used for fighting. Pirates and sailors used them for cutting ropes, canvass and wood.

The Message Bible says God's "powerful Word is sharp... cutting through everything, whether doubt or defence, laying us open to listen and obey. Nothing and no one is impervious to God's Word. We can't get away from it – no matter what."

The apostle Paul told the believers in Ephesus to "Put on the full armour of God... take the sword of the Spirit, which is the word of God." (Read Ephesians 6:10-18)

As we take God at His word and obey His commands we can move forward in His confidence – through any battle that comes our way in life.

Some years ago I wrote a song called "Two Edged Sword." The chorus proclaimed "Just like a shining two edged sword – your words cut deep in my heart. Making me see, that I must believe – what You say must come to pass. Your word of so old, and yet for today – I know will never fade away. Believe what God says, and then you will see – your hopes become reality."

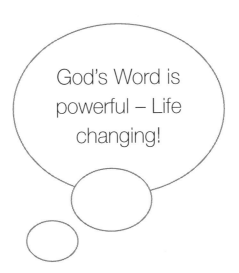

God's Word is powerful – Life changing!

God goes before us

My father use to be a Bank Manager. During his career, I recall a good number of occasions when the phone would ring in the middle of the night. It was the police, to say that the alarm was going off at the Bank. Dad would have to dress quickly and drive down to investigate. (It was helpful that we only lived a mile away)

Thankfully – each time Dad was called out, it was a false alarm. On arriving, Dad (being the Bank Employee) would have to open up and enter the building first.

As a youngster, I found this procedure hard to understand. My thinking was – if there was a burglar inside, the police ought to go in first to protect my Dad!

Are you facing a challenge or circumstance where you are stepping into the unknown – a situation you haven't experienced before?

Be encouraged by the words of the psalmist. In difficult times he proclaimed "In God I trust, I will not be afraid…" (Psalm 56:11)

He went on to say "God will go before me…" (Psalm 59:10) He knew that God was with him and for him.

When my Dad had to enter the Bank on the alarm calls – the police were behind him if he needed support.

The prophet Isaiah speaks of how God watches over His people – "for the Lord will go before you, the God of Israel will be your rearguard." (Isaiah 52:12)

God goes before – to lead us, but He also goes behind – keeping watch. King David put it like this: "You hem me in, behind and before; you have laid your hand upon me." (Psalm 139:5)

God goes before you – and is your rearguard

Peace within the storm

From our office window we can look across to Torquay, and then in the distance we can see Exmouth and Sidmouth.

As the "seagull flies" the distance between Brixham and Sidmouth is just over 23 miles, and over the years we've seen many different weather conditions over that area of sea. We have also observed rain storms coming across Torbay, and at times this has been a good advance warning to go and get the washing in from the line.

Matthew records in his gospel a time when Jesus and his disciples had got into a boat and "suddenly" there arose a violent storm on the sea, so that the boat was being covered up by the waves. Jesus was asleep in the boat.

His disciples awakened Him saying "Lord rescue us! We are perishing!" Jesus said to them "Why are you fearful, O you of little faith." (Matthew 8:23-27) Jesus rebuked the winds and the sea – and there was perfect peace.

Those times when things come upon us "suddenly" can be difficult to handle. We are taken by surprise as something totally unexpected enters into our day. Everything can be going well for us one minute – and then a situation can arise which turns our world upside down.

When we put our trust in God we have that assurance that He is with us all the time.

Moses reminded Israel in Deuteronomy 31:6 "your God goes with you; He will never leave you nor forsake you."

The "sudden" storm that hits your life – may take some time to be stilled – but you can experience the peace and presence of God "within" the storm.

Some years ago I wrote a song about this. The words go: "Every step I take the Lord is with me – and there's nowhere on the way that He will leave me – Knowing that His love will always lift me – above the burdens of the day. Lord: You are my Peace within the storm – You are my Healer when I'm torn."

God is with you
in the storm

Ready for life's journey

My wife and I wanted to visit our family in Cardiff. We decided to travel by train and started to make our journey arrangements in good time. An advertisement for British Rail some years ago used the slogan "Let the train take the strain."

Travelling by train enabled us to relax on our journey – but we still needed to prepare for our travel plans. We had to investigate train times, best fares, number of Station changes, order tickets and most importantly – check weather forecasts to see what clothes would have to be squeezed into our small suitcases!

Every day, each one of us is on the "journey of life" where we will need to make plans and preparations. Someone once said "When you fail to plan, you plan to fail."

On many occasions throughout the Bible – God called His people to times of preparation. Samuel spoke to the entire house of Israel saying "prepare your hearts for the Lord, and serve Him only: and he will deliver you from the hand of the Philistines."(1 Samuel 7:3)

God wants us to acknowledge Him in every circumstance of our lives – on every part of our journey.

God's call and plan for John the Baptist was to use his life and preaching… "to make ready a people prepared for the Lord." (Luke 1:16-17)

The Message Bible says "In a well-furnished kitchen there are not only crystal goblets and silver platters, but waste cans and compost buckets – some containers used to serve fine meals, others to take out the garbage. Become the kind of container God can use to present any and every kind of gift to his guests for their blessing." (2 Timothy 2:21)

As we choose and commit to live for God in this way, we will be prepared for every good work that He has planned for us.

Be prepared – take time to plan!

Foundations

We were having our garage rebuilt. The old one was a prefabricated construction and a number of concrete blocks in some sections had started to move! The builders commenced, and very soon the old garage was dismantled.

I hoped that the new garage was going to be built on the existing concrete base – but on further inspection, the builders advised that we would need new deeper foundations.

Foundations are unseen and take time to put down – but it is vital that they are laid correctly and are strong enough to take the weight of the building.

Once the foundation was completed the garage soon started to take shape as blocks and bricks were laid and roof support timbers went up.

The Bible refers to foundations. The Book of Proverbs tells us that "God marked out the foundations of the earth" and "By wisdom the Lord laid the earth's foundations..." (Proverbs 8:29b / 3:19)

The Psalmist said of God, "He set the earth on its foundations; it can never be moved." (Psalm 104:5)

When we experience difficult circumstances – it can feel like the foundation of our lives are being shaken. Isaiah the prophet reminds us that the Lord God "will be the sure foundation for your times, a rich store of salvation" (Isaiah 33:6)

Underneath the concrete of our new garage – layers of compacted hardcore stones were laid to strengthen the base. We can know God to be our Rock and strength when we make His Word the foundation for our lives.

David wrote in Psalm 40:1-2 "I waited patiently for the Lord; He turned to me and heard my cry. He lifted me out of the mud and mire; He set my feet on a rock and gave me a firm place to stand."

The God who laid the foundations of the world – is the One we can trust to help us stand firm when the going gets tough.

God is the sure foundation for our times

Power of Attorney

Before my mother died, she went through progressive dementia for over four years. She had already appointed me to be her Power of Attorney, and this enabled me to make decisions for her, as she became incapable of making them for herself.

When it came to buying clothes for Mum, choosing her food, deciding when household items needed replacing and finally what Care Home she should move to – I had to put myself in Mum's shoes and ask "What would Mum have chosen when she was able. What would she have liked?"- rather than let my personal choice influence decisions.

Stepping into "another person's shoes" (fully understanding what a person is going through and how they feel) requires us to have both sympathy and empathy towards them.

Sympathy is when we are aware of a person's distress or suffering, and have compassion on them. Empathy goes a step further: it expresses compassion, but also shows a deeper level of understanding, because "we've been there" and experienced the same difficulties.

The Bible reminds us that God has compassion towards us, and we are to show compassion to others.

God also fully understands how we feel. Jeremiah said "You understand, O Lord; remember me and care for me" (Jeremiah 15:15)

David wrote in his Psalm – "The Lord is gracious and compassionate, slow to anger and rich in love. The Lord is good to all; He has compassion on all he has made." (Psalm 145:8-9)

Jesus' brother James said – "The Lord is full of compassion and mercy." (James 5:11b)

The apostle Paul said to the Church at Colosse "clothe yourselves with compassion." (Colossians 3:12)

The experiences we have in life (especially the hard and complex ones) God can use – so that we can share and show compassion, kindness and sensitivity to others who are going through the same.

God understands you

Thorn in the hay

Just before Christmas I received two letters by post, both from well known major food stores. One wishes us Merry Christmas and adds "We've got Christmas all wrapped up". The other tells me "Christmas is a time for celebration, so why not indulge your family, your friends and yourself with some special treats…"

Whatever people may say or think about Christmas the truth is that the CHRIST of Christmas came into our world, and from Him all the kindness and all the truth of God has come down to us.

Several years ago I worked at a Holiday Farm complex. I recall one day, as I walked among the bundles of hay seeing a large thorn branch coming into the barn.

The bigger picture of why Jesus came to earth came to my mind.

The hay made me think of how Jesus was placed in a manger, because there was no room for Him at the inn and the thorn branch reminded me of the crown of thorns that was put on the head of Jesus when He was crucified to take away the sins of the world.

The baby Jesus in the Christmas manger is the Saviour Christ of the Good Friday Cross and the Risen, Living, Sovereign LORD of Easter Day.

At the first Christmas; Jesus' the true light that gives light to everyone came into the world. (John 1:9)

To all who believe in His name, He gives the right to become the children of God. (John 1:12)

God stepped down into our world in human form, and in Jesus you can experience His forgiveness, love, peace, joy, hope, healing and purpose in your life.

At this Christmas time, alongside any gifts you may be given from your family and friends, may you receive the most precious Gift of God which is eternal life in Jesus Christ our Lord.

God is with us –
His presence
within us